AF269674

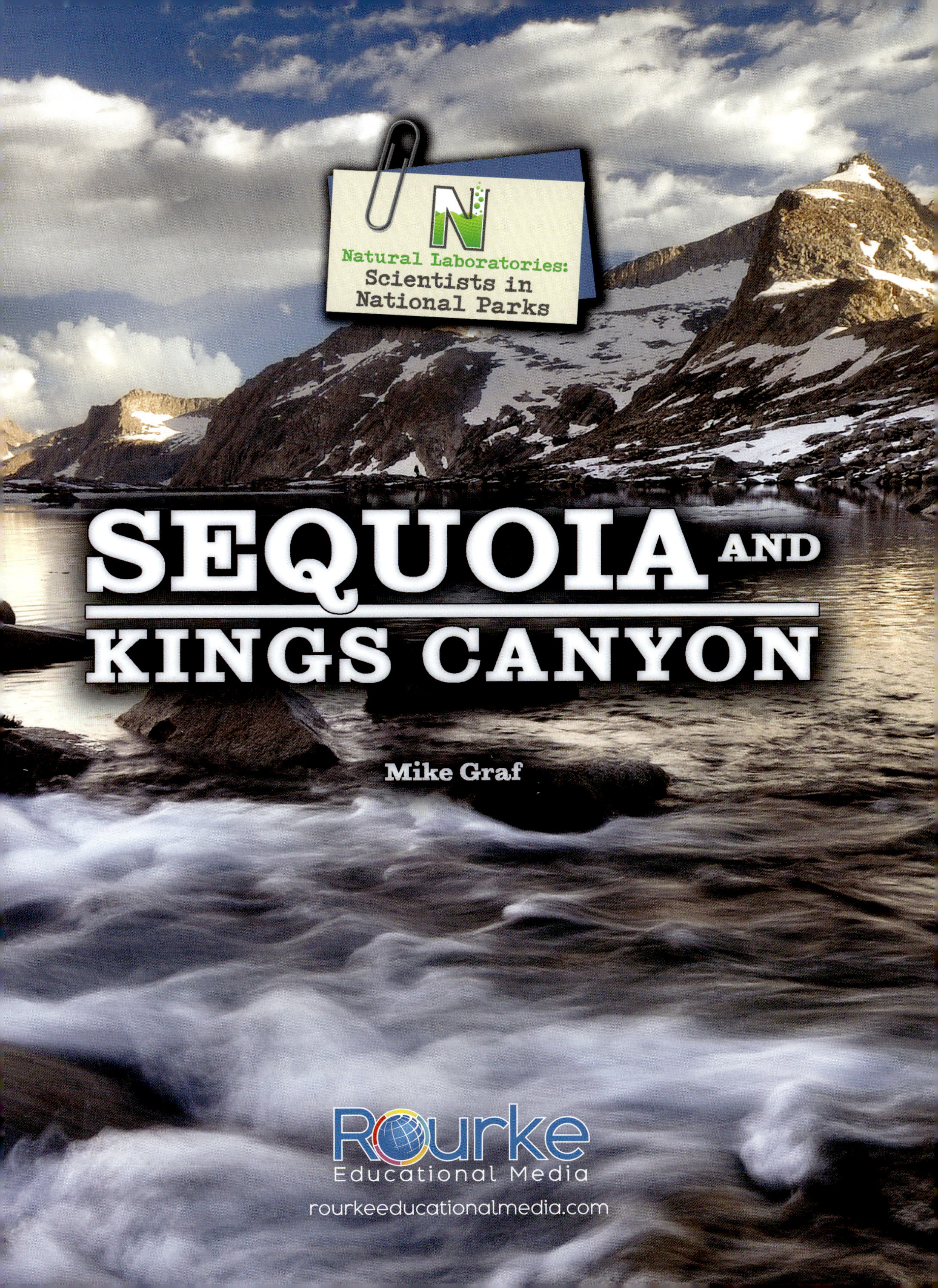

Natural Laboratories: Scientists in National Parks

SEQUOIA AND KINGS CANYON

Mike Graf

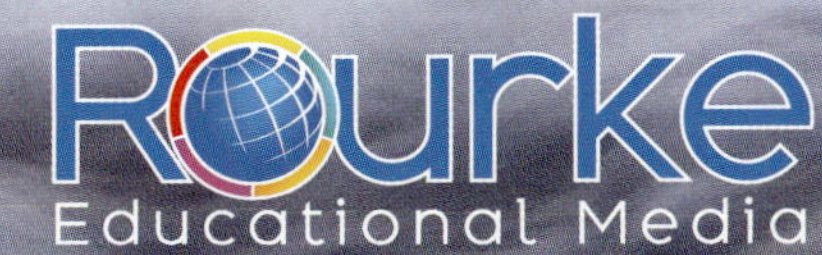

Rourke Educational Media
rourkeeducationalmedia.com

Before, During, and After Reading Activities

Before Reading: Building Background Knowledge and Academic Vocabulary

"Before Reading" strategies activate prior knowledge and set a purpose for reading. Before reading a book, it is important to tap into what your child or students already know about the topic. This will help them develop their vocabulary and increase their reading comprehension.

Questions and activities to build background knowledge:
1. *Look at the cover of the book. What will this book be about?*
2. *What do you already know about the topic?*
3. *Let's study the Table of Contents. What will you learn about in the book's chapters?*
4. *What would you like to learn about this topic? Do you think you might learn about it from this book? Why or why not?*

Building Academic Vocabulary

Building academic vocabulary is critical to understanding subject content.
Assist your child or students to gain meaning of the following vocabulary words.

Content Area Vocabulary

Read the list. What do these words mean?

- *carbonic acid*
- *climate*
- *contaminants*
- *gullies*
- *native*
- *nitrogen*
- *percolated*
- *petition*
- *regenerate*
- *runoff*
- *volume*

During Reading: Writing Component

"During Reading" strategies help to make connections, monitor understanding, generate questions, and stay focused.
1. *While reading, write in your reading journal any questions you have or anything you do not understand.*
2. *After completing each chapter, write a summary of the chapter in your reading journal.*
3. *While reading, make connections with the text and write them in your reading journal.*
   a) *Text to Self – What does this remind me of in my life? What were my feelings when I read this?*
   b) *Text to Text – What does this remind me of in another book I've read? How is this different from other books I've read?*
   c) *Text to World – What does this remind me of in the real world? Have I heard about this before? (News, current events, school, etc.…)*

After Reading: Comprehension and Extension Activity

"After Reading" strategies provide an opportunity to summarize, question, reflect, discuss, and respond to text. After reading the book, work on the following questions with your child or students to check their level of reading comprehension and content mastery.
1. *How have sequoia trees been protected? (Summarize)*
2. *How might sequoia trees survive in the future? (Infer)*
3. *Why did some people want to cut down sequoias? (Asking Questions)*
4. *What type of research would you be interested in doing at these parks if you were a scientist? (Text to Self Connection)*

Extension Activity

Is there a tree on your property or area that you think needs protecting? What is it about this particular tree that is so special? What does it provide for people, animals and insects, as well as other plants? Why might the tree be in danger of being removed? What can be done to protect that tree?

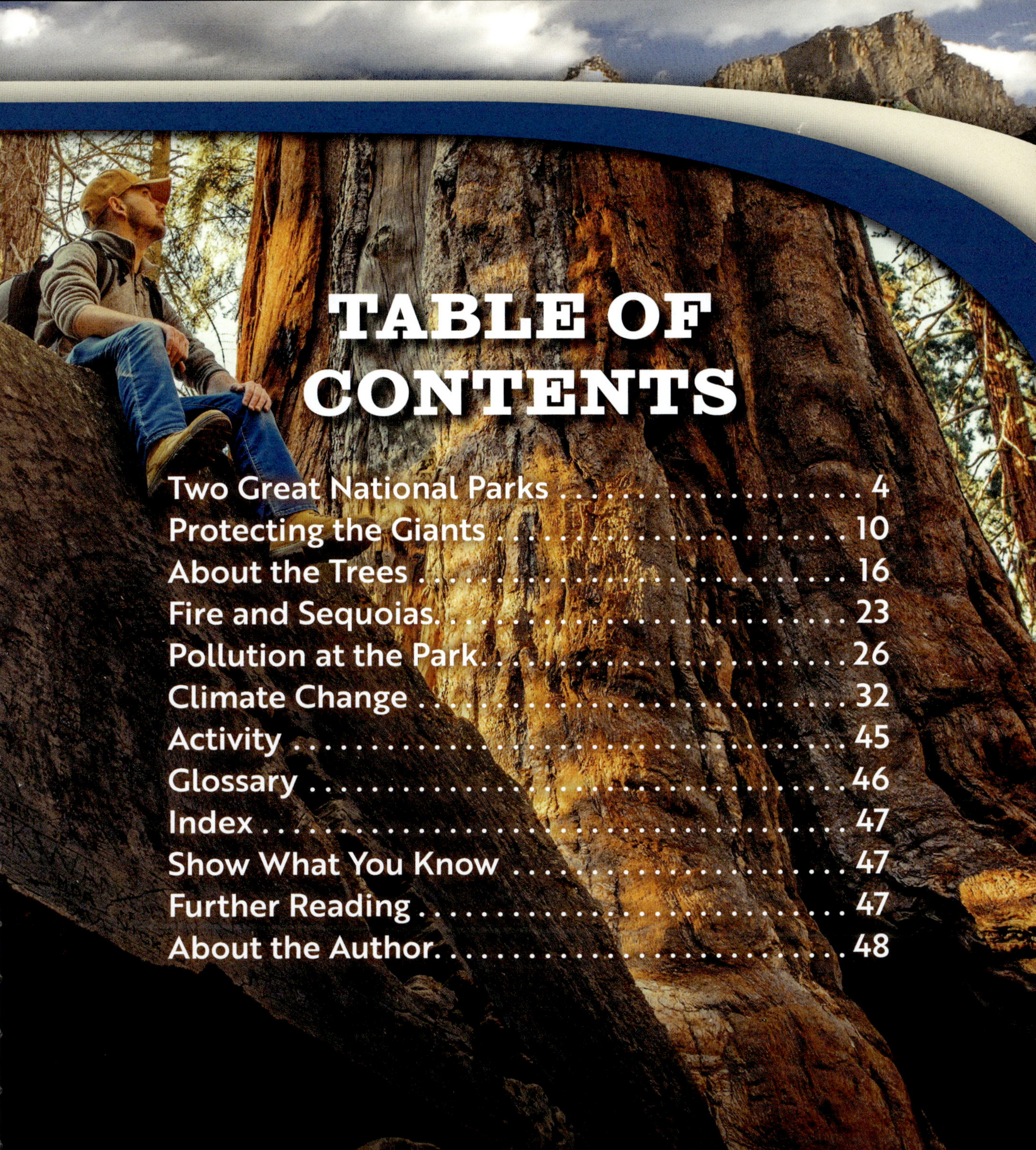

TABLE OF CONTENTS

CHAPTER ONE

TWO GREAT NATIONAL PARKS

Sequoia and Kings Canyon National Parks are right next to each other in California's Southern Sierra Nevada Mountains. The two parks feature giant sequoia trees, high mountains, deep canyons, and foothills.

The elevations at the two parks range from below 2,000 feet (610 meters) to high peaks over 14,000 feet (4,267 meters). This includes Mount Whitney, the highest peak in the United States outside of Alaska.

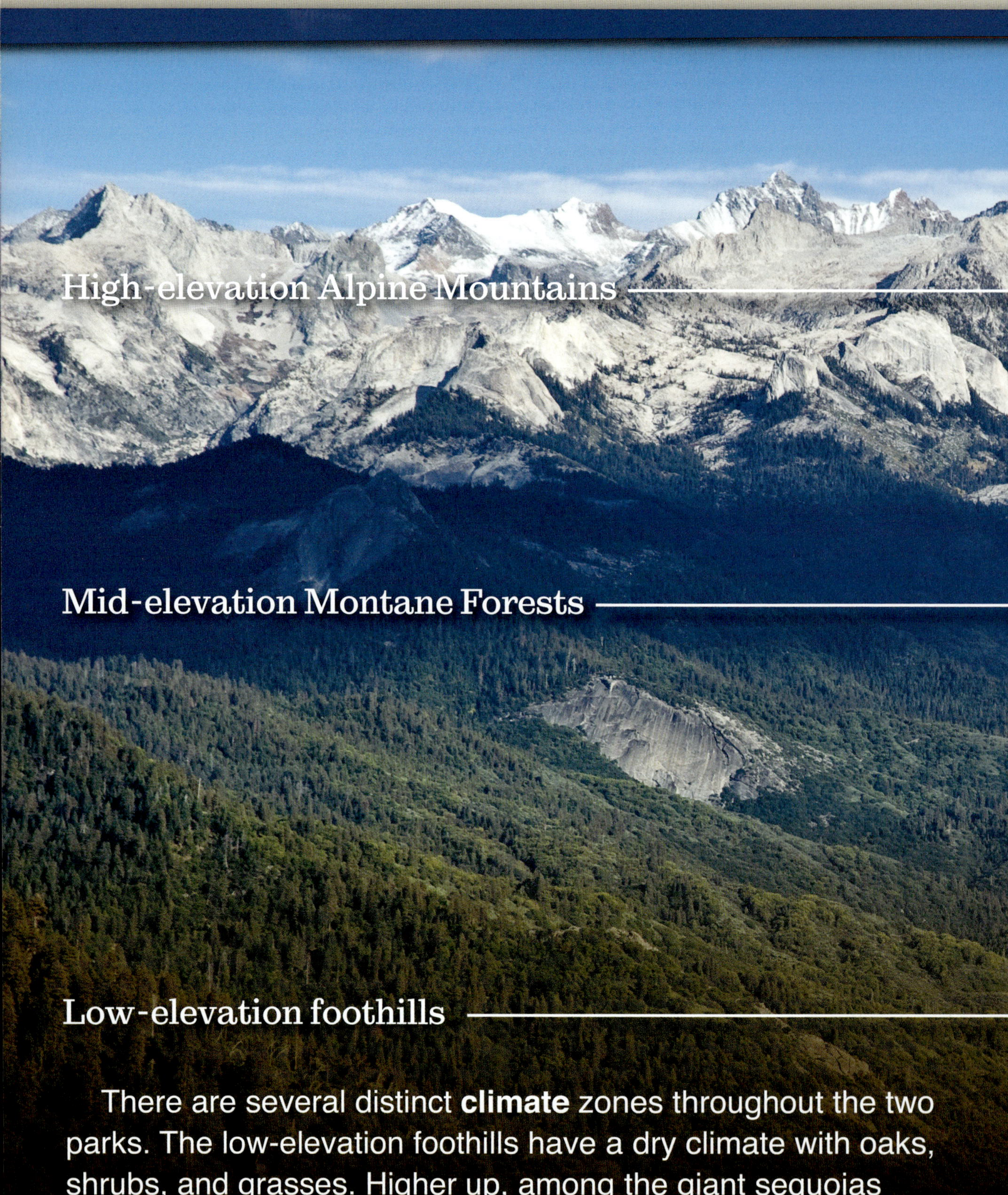

There are several distinct **climate** zones throughout the two parks. The low-elevation foothills have a dry climate with oaks, shrubs, and grasses. Higher up, among the giant sequoias there are warm summers, and cool, wet winters with snow.

The highest peaks have low-lying plants and a climate that is similar to the Arctic. It is cold in the high mountains most of the year.

The view from Moro Rock in Sequoia National Park

Sequoia and Kings Canyon are most known for their groves of giant sequoia trees. Sequoias are the largest living things in the world. The first widely reported sighting of a giant sequoia was by Augustus T. Dowd in 1852.

News of the trees spread, but some people called them the "California Hoax," saying no tree that large could really exist. Others marveled at sections of the trees that were taken to exhibits such as the Centennial Exhibition in Philadelphia in 1876. The 1,350-year-old Mark Twain Tree was cut down in 1891 and slabs of its trunk were shipped to museums in New York and London.

A section of the General Noble Tree was taken for display at the Columbian Exposition in Chicago in 1893. At the time this was the largest tree ever cut down.

Some of the largest trees, such as the Mark Twain Tree, are now just stumps, serving as reminders of how massive these giants once were.

PROTECTING THE GIANTS

Loggers were interested in the amount of wood a single sequoia could provide. However, the trees often shattered and fell apart as they hit the forest floor. In 1888, one of the loggers, Walter Fry, spent five days with a team of men sawing down a giant sequoia. He then counted the tree's growth by the rings in the trunk.

Many loggers were needed to fell each tree.

Walter Fry became an advocate for the trees, and helped protect them for the rest of his life. He eventually became a park ranger!

Fry realized that in just a few days he and his crew had ended 3,266 years of life! Two years later a **petition** went around asking for signatures to create a new national park. Fry's name was third on the list.

Hale Tharp first came to the Sequoia's Giant Forest in 1858. He was also an advocate to protect the trees. In 1861, Tharp built a small cabin right inside the end of a downed sequoia log. He grazed cattle in the grove's Crescent Meadow and lived in the cabin until 1890.

Tharp's Log is in the heart of the Giant Forest.

Both Tharp and John Muir, one of the world's most famous conservationists, were inspired by the massive trees. Muir wrote that the grove of sequoias in the Giant Forest was the finest he had ever seen. Because of Fry, Tharp, Muir and others, on September 25, 1890, Sequoia became the second national park in the United States.

part of the Giant Forest, Sequoia National Park

In the early 1900s, a photographer named Susan Thew spent several summers around the park to photograph and publish pictures of the beauty and serenity of the sequoias. Thew's photographic records were sent to the United States Congress. This led to the expansion of Sequoia National Park.

Susan Thew took many of her photographs in the southern Sierra Nevada.

Nearby Grant Grove National Park also protected a strand of giant sequoias. On March 4, 1940, that park was renamed and increased in size to make Kings Canyon National Park.

"Conservationists like Susan Thew provide continuing inspiration for those of us who came after her. Knowing the incredible effort that Ms. Thew undertook to protect these parks reminds us to always keep conservation in mind and not take short cuts in our preservation efforts." — Christy Brigham Ph. D., Chief of Resources Management and Science

General Grant tree in Grant Grove

CHAPTER THREE

ABOUT THE TREES

Sequoia trees only live naturally in California's central and southern Sierra Nevada Mountains. There are about 75 groves left. Sequoias favor an elevation range from 4,000 to 8,000 feet (1,219 to 2,438 meters). They thrive in locations that have cool wet winters with snow, and warm dry summers. Many of the giant trees live near a year-round water source such as a creek, meadow, or stream.

Sequoias are related to two other living trees, the coast redwood, which grows along the northern California coast and in Southern Oregon, and the dawn redwood, which grows in isolated regions of China.

Winter is an especially beautiful time to visit the sequoia forest.

Five of the ten largest trees in the world are in the Giant Forest in Sequoia National Park. The General Sherman Tree, the world's largest sequoia, is one of them.

Both trees reach for the sky. But redwoods are often taller, and sequoias are wider, making sequoias the larger tree overall.

There are more than 2,000 other large sequoias in the Giant Forest. Sequoia trees can grow up to 300 feet (91 meters) tall. Coast redwoods grow taller, but sequoias are much bulkier at their base, making them the world's largest tree by **volume**.

We are very small when looking at a giant sequoia. To see them in person is incredible!

Sequoias can grow a very long time, some living more than three thousand years! Scientists determine the age of trees by counting the number of rings in their trunks. This type of science is known as dendrochronology. Each year a tree is alive, the tree grows a new ring.

Each year this tree was alive it grew a new ring. The center of the trunk has the oldest rings.

This sequoia's rings shows it was more than 2,000 years old when it was cut down.

Scientists climb a sequoia to study it and to get a ring sample.

Scientists in the park use ring samples to learn whether the trees are stressed. The samples are taken from the trees 33 feet (10 meters) off the ground so the sequoias are not harmed.

Once viewed these ring samples tell scientists whether the tree's growth has slowed down because of the drought.

Increment Borers

A tool called an increment borer is used for collecting ring samples from trees. On sequoias this is done higher up to protect the tree and stop it from losing water.

CHAPTER FOUR

FIRE AND SEQUOIAS

The area around Sequoia is hot and dry during the summer and fires are common. Until the early 1960's, it was National Park Service policy to put out all fires to protect structures, visitors, and the giant trees.

Scientists now know that fires help sequoias. Fires open up cones, which allow seeds to come out.

A single giant sequoia can drop thousands of cones.
Each cone has hundreds of seeds.

Fires also clear out areas for sequoias to grow and provide **nitrogen** to the soil, which fertilizes it.

Because it used to be policy to put out all fires, regeneration of baby sequoia trees was rare. Now fires are prescribed or purposely started in some locations to help **regenerate** sequoias.

Natural fire scars are pointed out in this sequoia tree's trunk.

Scientists are happy to report that new sequoias are growing again!
Redwood Mountain
1485
1464
1480
1507
1543
1558
1522
1570
1590
1611
1627
1652
1684

CHAPTER FIVE

POLLUTION AT THE PARK

Just below Sequoia and Kings Canyon is California's San Joaquin Valley. This region is full of farms. Many trucks hauling goods on crowded freeways add pollution to the air.

Exhaust from trucks on crowded freeways adds to the air pollution in the area.

The region also gets what is called a "Fresno Eddy" weather pattern. Polluted air is blown southeast from the San Francisco Bay Area toward the Tehachapi Mountains south of the park. The air is then circulated back up to the mountains of Sequoia and Kings Canyon in a repeated pattern. All this contributes to some of the worst air pollution in the United States.

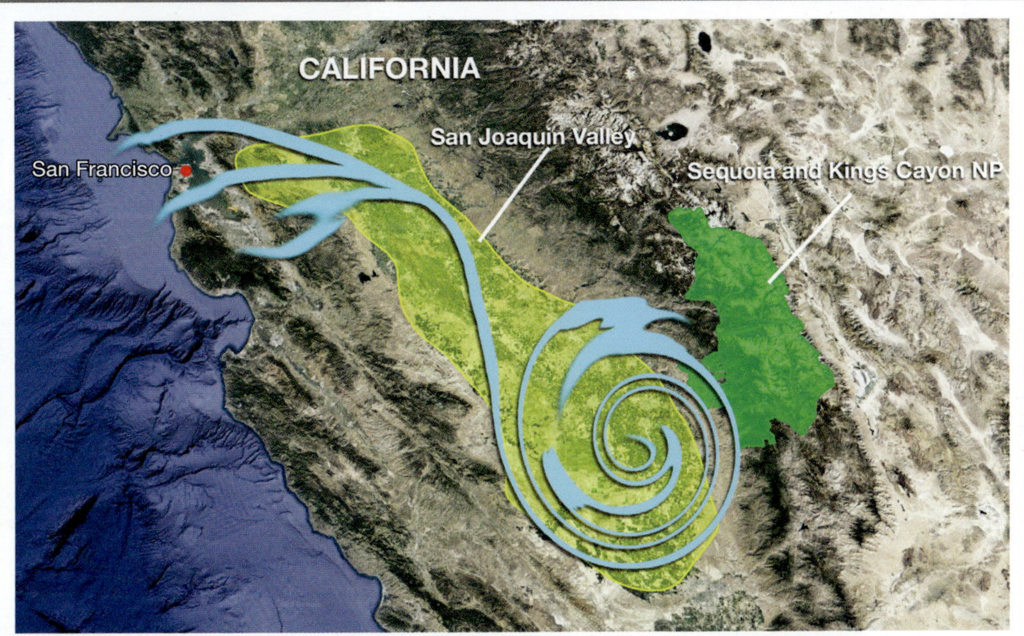

The Fresno Eddy air pattern traps pollution up against the mountains of Sequoia and Kings Canyon National Parks.

Smoggy air reduces visibility in the Kings Canyon Mountains.

Scientists are studying how the poor air quality affects giant sequoias. Mature giant sequoia trees appear to be tolerant to pollution and undamaged. But seedlings are more vulnerable to ozone, which is air pollution in the lower atmosphere.

An air quality technician checks equipment at a Sequoia National Park monitoring site.

Haze from air pollution and smoke is common in Sequoia and Kings Canyon National Parks.

Sequoia seedlings are more vulnerable than full-grown trees to pollution and less likely to survive.

Ozone

O₃

Ozone is a colorless, toxic gas and also a pollutant in the lower atmosphere.

Upper photo shows example of healthy Jeffrey pine needles and lower photo shows needles with yellowing (or chlorotic mottlling) as a result of ozone effects.

"Ozone is entering into sequoia seedlings' leaf systems and acting as a corrosive gas. This turns the seedling's needles yellow. This is called chlorotic mottle. These seedlings are now injured, more vulnerable, and less likely to survive." — Annie Esperanza, Air Resources Specialist and Branch Chief for Physical Sciences

Park scientists are finding **contaminants** in the park. These harmful substances have gotten into creeks, rivers, lakes, and snow, as well as some wildlife. Some of the pollutants are brought in by people who swim or wade in the water. Others are brought in by the wind and drop from the atmosphere. Scientists have found mercury, DEET, medications, and some pesticides in the water.

Water and soil samples are tested for contaminants by scientists at the park.

Mercury is a naturally
occurring element found in
Earth's crust. It is highly toxic
and gets into the atmosphere by
the burning of coal, oil, and wood.

The Greatest Danger

According to park scientists, mercury is the pollutant of greatest concern. Dragonfly larvae, fish, turtles, water and snow are studied to see how much mercury has accumulated in the food web. If mercury levels become too high, wildlife health could be impacted. Also, people will be advised to not eat fish caught from park waters.

National Park Service scientists work with water and snow deposition monitoring equipment at Sequoia National Park.

Emerald Lake is one of two lakes sampled in Sequoia National Park for airborne contaminants.

CLIMATE CHANGE

The normal precipitation season at Sequoia and Kings Canyon is November to April. That is when most of the parks' rain and snow falls. A great deal of the park is at high elevation—above 6,000 feet (1,829 meters). Much of what falls up there is snow.

Precipitation is much more common in winter and early spring at the two parks.

Now, due to climate change, more rain is falling and less snow. Droughts are also more common. Smaller snowpack means less **runoff** in creeks and rivers, especially during the dry months of summer.

The dead trees in the distance are a sign of a long-term drought in the park.

Pikas are small, furry mammals that only live at high elevations where it stays cool all year. They gather and stockpile grasses in the summer. In the winter, they live on what they found during the short growing season. If the summer temperatures go above 70 degrees Fahrenheit (21 degrees Celsius), pikas get stressed and try to find shade. If the warm weather continues, they may not be able to forage for enough food to last the winter.

A haypile of food gathered by a pika for eating during the winter.

Pikas live among rocks where crevices can help keep them cool.

Because of climate change there are fewer high elevation places cool enough for the pika. It is uncertain how pikas will respond to future climatic changes. They may find less range available as a suitable habitat, or they may find microclimates in their existing habitat and do just fine.

Researchers look for piles of fresh scat to determine if pikas are present.

There are more than 275 caves in Sequoia and Kings Canyon. The parks' caves are made of marble. They formed over millions of years as rainwater, mixed with **carbonic acid** got in the water and **percolated** into the rock. This acidic water dissolved the marble into caves. Scientists are monitoring if less water and warmer temperatures above the caves are having any effect on them.

Spot temperatures are taken with handheld instruments.

Water and carbonic acid are the main two ingredients that carve the caves at the parks.

The little brown bat is one species of
bats that live in the caves.

The Crystal Cave millipede on
roots in the Rapunzels Canyon
of Crystal Cave

"The caves at Sequoia and Kings Canyon are some of the most biologically diverse in California. We are finding more living things here than many other California caves including mammals, birds, spiders, and insects such as crickets and millipedes. But with less water and warmer temperatures, we are concerned this could affect the living things inside the caves. Water quality due to pollution is also a concern." — Annie Esperanza, Air Resources Specialist and Branch Chief for Physical Sciences

Sequoia and Kings Canyon have several beautiful, lush meadows. In the heart of the Giant Forest are Crescent Meadow, Round Meadow and Long Meadow. Kings Canyon has Zumwalt Meadow and many other lovely high-elevation meadows.

Meadows get their water from precipitation and groundwater. But with less precipitation and warmer temperatures, park meadows may dry out more than normal during the summer.

Sequoia National Park's fallen "Tunnel Log" is located along Crescent Meadow Road in the Giant Forest.

Crescent Meadow at beginning of summer

Zumwalt Meadow in Kings Canyon National Park

Crescent Meadow at end of summer

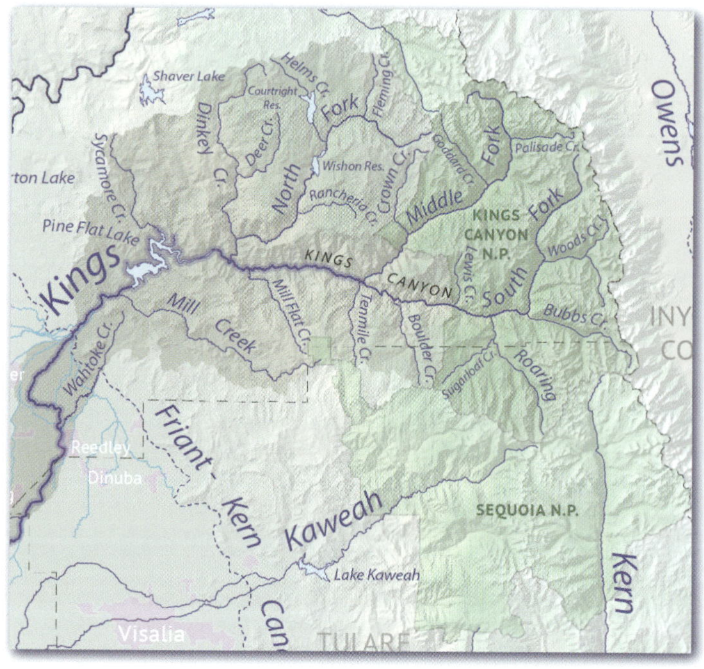

Cahoon Meadow has been severely damaged in the past by grazing practices and erosion gullies. Some parts of the meadow have been completely drained of water.

Some of the meadows in the park have had cattle grazing and other human activities in the past. Ditches and **gullies** were dug back then, diverting water from the meadows.

The Kings River runs through much of Kings Canyon National Park.

This area of the meadow is unaffected.

Rangers and scientists are trying to prevent these meadows from further drying out. The ditches and gullies are being removed so the natural water flow can return.

Crews place erosion control blankets under new grasses.

The combination of stress from drought and attack by **native** bark beetles are killing trees throughout the Western United States, including the parks. The beetles eat the inner bark of trees, which cuts off the flow of nutrients and eventually kills the trees. Bark beetles are spreading due to warmer weather and they thrive during droughts.

Park scientists are using prescribed fires to maintain a diverse, healthy forest which they hope will be more resistant to the beetles.

A prescribed burn in Kings Canyon

A combination of drought and
beetle damage kills pine trees.

They are also
applying pheromones
onto sugar pines in
busy areas such as
Grant Grove of Kings
Canyon. This chemical
application sends
a message to bark
beetles that the tree is
already inhabited by
other beetles and they
leave it alone.

A forestry worker applies a dollop of pheromone to a park tree.

Scientists have been working at Sequoia and Kings Canyon National Parks for more than 100 years. They will continue to study how to best protect the parks. What Sequoia and Kings Canyon will be like in the future depends on continuing research and conservation efforts.

Citizen Scientists

The two parks have many opportunities for volunteers to help! School groups and others work with scientists in collecting data on trees, water, animals, and gathering dragonfly larvae. Volunteers also pull invasive weeds from meadows to help restore their natural beauty.

BE A TREE SCIENTIST

Sequoia and Kings Canyon are known for the largest trees on Earth. They are also some of the oldest! Scientists can determine a tree's age by its rings. But how do you find out how old a tree is without cutting it down?

Supplies

- tape measure
- notebook and pen
- resource books
- internet access

Directions:

1. Choose a tree in your neighborhood or at school to measure. Determine what species the tree is using books or by searching the internet.

2. Wrap a tape measure around the tree at about four and a half feet (1.4 meters) above the ground. This is the tree's circumference. Record this measurement.

3. Using a calculator, divide this measurement by 3.14. This will give you the tree's diameter.

4. Using the internet, find the growth factor of the tree by searching the species name and "growth factor." Multiply your tree's diameter by this number. This will give you the tree's approximate age.

Glossary

carbonic acid (KAHR-bon-ik AS-id): a weak acid formed by the remains of plants and animals that when combined with water can dissolve certain rocks over a long period of time

climate (KLYE-mit): the general weather conditions of an area over a long period of time

contaminants (kuhn-TAM-uh-nints): polluting or poisonous substances

gullies (guh-lees): ravines or ditches that water travels through

native (NAY-tiv): a plant or animal that originates from a particular area

nitrogen (NYE-truh-juhn): a chemical agent found in the atmosphere and in animal and plant matter often used as a fertilizer

percolated (pur-KOH-layt-id): when liquid filtered through or permeated a soil and rock layer

petition (puh-TISH-uhn): a written, formal request signed by many people and sent to authorities regarding a particular matter

regenerate (re-JEN-uh-rate): to grow again in partial such as a crab regenerating a claw or in full such as new trees in a grove

runoff (RUHN-awf): the draining away of water from a surface area of land

volume (VAHL-yoom): the amount of space an object occupies

Index

Show What You Know

1. Why didn't people believe at first that sequoias were real?
2. How did people find out how old a sequoia was?
3. How do fires help sequoias?
4. How is climate change affecting the two parks?
5. Which area of Sequoia Park is most interesting to you and why?

Further Reading

Graf, Mike, *Secrets of the Sequoias: Adventures with the Parkers,* Farcountry Press, 2016.

Martin Weyand, Mary, *Of Giants and Grizzlies,* Write On For Kids, 2015.

National Park Notebooks, *Sequoia National Park Junior Notebook,* 2018.

About the Author

Mike Graf is the author of more than 90 nonfiction and fiction books for children, teachers, and families. He speaks at schools and conferences all over the United States. Mike lives in Northern California with his wife and daughter. In their free time they love to travel, hike, and enjoy the outdoors in as many ways as possible. You can learn more about Mike at www.mikegrafauthor.com.

www.rourkeeducationalmedia.com

PHOTO CREDITS: Cover foreground photo and contents page © welcomia2, title page and background photo on cover © Sierralara, card with paper clip art © beths; page 4 Mount Whitney © Zhukova Valentyna, page 4-5 and 13 trees © welcomia; page 6-7 © Anatoliy Lukich, page 8 © My Good Images; page 12-13 cabin © Deatonphotos; page 15 © Mark52; page 16 relief map © Schwabenblitz, U.S. map © Globe Turner, page 17 © Pung; pages 18-19 © Nick Fox, page 19 General Sherman tree © haveseen, redwood trees © Min C. Chiu; page 20-21 scientist in tree large photo © Candia Baxter; cut away of Sequoia © Kris Wiktor, smaller photo of cutaway © Bildagentur Zoonar GmbH; page 23 fire background photo © Jared Simeth; P26-27 crossover photo © rhettstuart, truck photo © vitpho, mountains © Pierdelune, ; page 29 molecule © honglouwawa; P30 © Ivan Chudakov; Page 34-35 large photo of pika © South 500 Photography; page 36 main photo © ckchiu, bottom inset photo © Orchid24; page 38 meadow looking green © urosr, unnel log © mhgstan, page 39 meadow looking brown © Serj Malomuzh, mountain photo © Benny Marty, t; page 42-43 full page photo © Michael Vi, inset of pine trees page 42-43 © keldridge; page 44 © Photodiem, page 45 photo © Anna Dorokhov, leaf sketches © Linda Brotkorb. All images from Shutterstock.com except page 5 map courtesy of NPS; page 9 Mark Twain stump: Daniels, Gene, photographer, source National Archives, page 9 black and white photo public domain; page 10 Walter Fry courtesy of NPS, 10-11 courtesy of Library of Congress; page 13 John Muir public domain; page 14 photos courtesy of NPS; page 21 scientist in tree smaller photo courtesy Anthony Ambrose UC Berkeley, page 22 tree ring sampling courtesy Peter M. Brown, Rocky Mountain Tree-Ring Research; page 23 pinecone courtesy Alex Demas, USGS; page 24-25 crossover photo courtesy of NPS Sequoia and Kings Canyon NP, page 25 inset photo courtesy of NPS; page 27 map © C. Lopetz; pages 28 top inset photo courtesy of NPS, bottom inset photo © Rmiramontes I istockphoto.com, bottom photo showing forest and bottom inset photo on page 29 courtesy of NPS, top photo page 29 © Ozone Pix © undefined undefined I istockphoto.com; page 31 mercury © MarcelClemen I istockphoto.com, page 31 bottom inset photos courtesy of the NPS; page 32-33 crossover photo © robertcicchetti istockphoto.com, graph © Goldilock Project, inset photo page 33 waymoreawesomer I istockphoto.com; page 34-35 American pika with twig © Dcrjsr https://creativecommons.org/licenses/by/3.0/deed.en; dried grass © Chrharshaw https://creativecommons.org/licenses/by/3.0/deed.en;, scat photo courtesy of NPS; page 36 top inset photo courtesy of NPS; page 37 brown bats courtesy of USFWS, millipede NPS photo by Joel Despain; page 40-41 all photos courtesy of NPS except map © Shannon1 https://creativecommons.org/licenses/by-sa/4.0/; page 43 inset photo of beetle courtesy of NPS, inset photo of forest courtesy of Nathan Stephenson USGS, bottom inset photo page 43 courtesy of U.S. Forest Service;

Edited by: Keli Sipperley

Produced by Blue Door Education for Rourke Educational Media. Cover design and page layout by: Nicola Stratford

Sequoia and Kings Canyon / Mike Graf
(Natural Laboratories: Scientists in National Parks)
ISBN 978-1-64369-026-1 (hard cover)
ISBN 978-1-64369-111-4 (soft cover)
ISBN 978-1-64369-173-2 (e-Book)
Library of Congress Control Number: 2018956043

Printed in the United States of America, North Mankato, Minnesota